GEORGE *Washington*

GEORGE *Washington*

OUR FIRST PRESIDENT

By Ann Graham Gaines

SPIRIT
of America™

The Child's World®, Inc.
Chanhassen, Minnesota

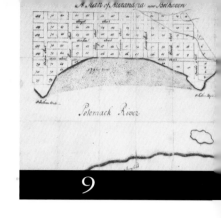

GEORGE *Washington*

Published in the United States of America by The Child's World®, Inc.
PO Box 326 • Chanhassen, MN 55317-0326 • 800-599-READ • www.childsworld.com

Acknowledgments

The Creative Spark: Mary Francis-DeMarois, Project Director; Elizabeth Sirimarco Budd, Series Editor; Robert Court, Design and Art Direction; Janine Graham, Page Layout; Jennifer Moyers, Production

The Child's World®, Inc.: Mary Berendes, Publishing Director; Red Line Editorial, Fact Research; Cindy Klingel, Curriculum Advisor; Robert Noyed, Historical Advisor

Photos

Cover: George Washington by Gilbert Stuart. Gift of Jean McGinley Draper. Photograph © 2000 Board of Trustees, National Gallery of Art, Washington; © Archivo Iconografico, S.A./CORBIS: 22; The Library of Congress Collection: 9, 10, 12, 15, 17, 24, 26, 27, 34, 35; The Metropolitan Museum of Art, gift of Edgar William and Bernice Chrysler Garbisch, 1963 (63.201.2): 30; The National Archives: 14; Independence National Historical Park: 6, 7, 16, 18, 19, 23 (left and right), 28; Courtesy of the National Museum of the American Indian, Smithsonian Institution (22/8915): 29; © Collection of The New-York Historical Society: 21; Wolfgang Kaehler/CORBIS: 32

Library of Congress Cataloging-in-Publication Data
Gaines, Ann.
  George Washington : our first president / by Ann Graham Gaines.
    p. cm.
  Includes index.
  ISBN 1-56766-842-9 (alk. paper)
  1. Washington, George, 1732–1799—Juvenile literature. 2. Presidents—United States—
Biography—Juvenile literature. [1. Washington, George, 1732–1799. 2. Presidents.] I. Title.
  E312.66 .G3 2001

                              00-010573

Contents

Chapter ONE	A Soldier's Life	6
Chapter TWO	Unanimous Vote	16
Chapter THREE	The Experiment	22
Chapter FOUR	A Second Term	28
	Time Line	36
	Glossary Terms	38
	Our Presidents	42
	Presidential Facts	46
	For Further Information	47
	Index	48

A Soldier's Life

Before he became the first American president, George Washington was a military hero, honored for his courage and skill on the battlefield.

GEORGE WASHINGTON NEVER WANTED TO BE the first president of the United States, even though Americans believed he was the perfect person to fill such an important role. What he wanted to do most was to be a farmer, just as his father had been. George Washington was born on February 22, 1732. As an adult, he owned a huge **plantation** and an elegant house. But Washington was not born rich. His father, Augustine, was an ordinary, hardworking man. As a little boy, George Washington probably helped him with farm chores.

By the time he was 11, Washington's family had begun to prosper. They lived on Ferry Farm, along the Rappahannock River in Virginia. Like many colonists at the time, especially in the South, the Washingtons owned slaves.

Washington was a big, strong boy. He loved the outdoors and was good at playing ball. He was an excellent horseman and spent much of his time roaming his family's land. He explored the woods and streams. Sometimes he rode a ferry across the river to visit the town of Fredericksburg. As an adult, Washington would remain an adventurous outdoorsman. He also enjoyed quiet, indoor pastimes, such as playing the flute, writing both letters and entries to his journal, and collecting paintings.

Washington's father, Augustine, was married twice. His second wife, Mary Bell Washington (above), was George's mother. Her grandfather settled in America in 1650.

When Augustine Washington died in 1743, George went to live with his half-brother, Lawrence. Lawrence owned a plantation called Mount Vernon. This lovely farm sat on the banks of the Potomac River. While living at Ferry Farm, Washington had learned his lessons from his parents. But Lawrence sent him to a regular school with other students and a teacher. This tiny school would be the end of George Washington's education. His family never had enough money to send him to college.

▶ People who want to teach children the value of honesty often tell a story about George Washington. In this story, he chopped down his father's cherry tree. When his father asked who did it, young Washington immediately confessed, "I can't tell a lie, Pa; you know I can't tell a lie. I did cut it with my hatchet." Actually, this never happened. A biographer named Mason Weems made it up for a book, *The Life of George Washington,* published in 1800. What is true is that George Washington valued honesty very highly.

Washington once went with neighbors to the Shenandoah Valley. They traveled there to make a map of land they had bought on the frontier. On this journey, Washington realized that he loved being out in the wilderness. He also was quite good at making maps.

When Washington reached age 16, he was nearly full grown. He was a huge man for his day and stood more than six feet tall. It was time for him to start earning his own living, just like other colonists his age. He eagerly accepted a job as a **surveyor.** This job would send him to the far West, the land beyond the Blue Ridge Mountains. Washington started to buy land of his own with the money he earned. He also loved to spend money on fine clothing and furniture. He purchased the very best items he could find.

In 1752, Lawrence Washington died. After Lawrence's widow died in 1761, George inherited Mount Vernon. Soon he took over his half-brother's position in the Virginia **militia.** Lawrence had been in charge of training all the volunteers who served in the colony's militia. George Washington quickly learned the skills of a soldier.

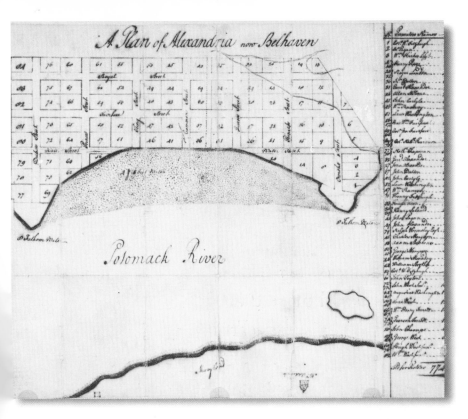

George Washington was trained as a surveyor during his teenage years. He worked on at least 150 maps during his lifetime. When he was 16 years old, Washington prepared this map of Alexandria, Virginia.

When he was just 21 years old, Virginia leaders asked Washington to lead an **expedition** to the Ohio River valley, where the king of England had given a group of Virginians a large piece of land. The problem was that the French were trying to settle there, too. Washington rode hard through rain and snow to reach the valley. When he arrived, he saw that the French had built a fort on British land.

Washington returned to tell Virginia leaders the bad news. The British and the American colonists decided to fight the French for these western lands. The French

George Washington carried both a sword and a rifle during the French and Indian War. The medallion he wore around his neck signified that he was an officer.

joined forces with their Native American **allies,** and the French and Indian War began.

Much of the war was fought in the wild, often in terrible, cold weather. Yet Washington returned home unwounded and in good health. He became a hero in the French and Indian War. In fact, he was placed in command of the whole Virginia militia. It was then that the colonists first recognized Washington's skillful military leadership.

At the end of the war, Washington returned to his plantation. Soon he married a widow named Martha Custis. Martha had two young children. She was a small, quiet woman who helped George Washington enjoy his time at home. Washington still loved to be outdoors. He would always be a superb horseman who enjoyed hunting. He liked to work on his farms. He did some experimenting with plants and trees and tried to grow new crops. Martha brought 15,000 acres of farmland into their marriage. She also had money that they used to buy even more property. George Washington was now a rich man.

Washington's fellow colonists respected him. He was elected four times as a **representative** to Virginia's House of Burgesses. This was the group of people who made laws for the colony. He became well known for being thoughtful and thorough. He did have a temper, but he tried hard to keep it under control. George Washington cared a great deal about what other people thought of him.

Over time, the British began to tax their American colonies more and more. Many colonists, including Washington, began to talk of fighting back. At first, they only wanted to make England stop taxing them so much. Later, they decided the colonies should break away from Britain. "The crisis is arrived," wrote Washington, "when we must assert our rights." Virginians elected Washington as one of the representatives to the colonies' **Continental Congress.**

People described Martha Washington as "simple, easy, and dignified." Throughout her life, she was steady and hardworking, a perfect companion for the nation's first president.

The Continental Congress appointed Washington general of the American army. He left Virginia for Massachusetts to take command.

In April of 1775, the British learned that Americans were preparing for war. The colonists had stockpiled gunpowder in Concord, Massachusetts. British soldiers marched there, planning to seize the Americans' **ammunition.** It was then that the first battles of the American **Revolution** broke out. Soon afterward, the **Continental Army** was organized. Americans considered Washington a fearless soldier and a good leader, so Congress named him general of the new army. He wrote to his wife, saying he had

12

accepted the job: "I have used every endeavor in my power to avoid it … but a kind of destiny … has thrown me upon this service.… It was utterly out of my power to refuse."

Washington told Congress that he would take the assignment "at the expense of my … ease and happiness." He refused to accept pay because he did not want to make any profit from the war. At first, Washington fought simply because he wanted the British to leave the American colonies alone. Later he believed his army was fighting for "the right of all people to govern themselves without outside interference." In other words, he believed that in their struggle for independence, the American colonies were fighting on behalf of colonists all over the world.

George Washington commanded the Continental Army for eight years. He proved a great commander. At times, he had to convince other Americans to keep fighting, even if it seemed they would lose. He inspired his soldiers with his courage and dedication. Often, his army was at a disadvantage. They had fewer men and supplies than the enemy. Sometimes his men were

▶ George Washington only took one trip outside America in his entire life. In 1751, he sailed to Barbados with his half-brother, Lawrence. They went there because Lawrence had a serious illness and hoped the island's tropical climate would help cure him.

▶ Once during the French and Indian War, the enemy shot Washington's horse out from under him. By the battle's end, he had four bullet holes in his uniform, but he had not been hurt. He became known as a very brave man.

On Christmas Eve in 1776, Washington and his men boarded boats in the middle of the night. They crossed the icy Delaware River in the dark to reach the enemy's camp. In a surprise attack, the Americans won the Battle of Trenton. It was their first victory. Winning the battle helped encourage them to continue their fight for independence.

cold and hungry. Washington always shared his soldiers' hardships.

At the beginning of the war, the British forced Washington's army to **retreat** from Massachusetts into Pennsylvania. But he fought back. Finally, after a year and a half of fighting, the Continental Army won their first battle on Christmas Eve, 1776.

By 1780, the American army was again in trouble. There had been more victories, but they were running short of food, shoes, and other supplies. Finally, France joined the war to help the Americans. Together, the Americans and French were able to beat the British. On October 19, 1781, British General Cornwallis **surrendered** at Yorktown.

Washington's army did not disband for two more years. The United States and Britain finally signed a peace **treaty** in September of 1783. Washington held his position until the British army left the country in November. Then he retired from his **commission** as commander of the Continental Army. He had spent eight years away from home. A grateful nation thanked him.

AS A GROWN MAN, GEORGE WASHINGTON LIVED AT MOUNT VERNON, a huge plantation that stretched for miles along the Potomac River in Virginia. He ran five separate farms on his land.

When Washington inherited it, Mount Vernon had only a modest house. He returned to Virginia after the Revolutionary War to a home with tiny rooms and walls that had been built nearly 100 years earlier. Still, he was thrilled to be at Mount Vernon again. "I am to become a private citizen on the banks of the Potomac," wrote Washington. "Free from the busy scenes of public life, I am retiring within myself."

Washington immediately set out to improve the house and make it more beautiful. He began by tearing down the walls to make bigger rooms. He designed the grounds around the mansion to include a forest border, meadows, walkways, and orchards. Between the mansion and the shores of the Potomac River was a park. The grounds also included both a pleasure garden and a kitchen garden. Eventually, Washington's home became one of the most elegant houses in the United States. Mount Vernon has changed very little over the last 200 years. Today the estate is very much as George Washington designed it.

Chapter TWO

Unanimous Vote

After the surrender at Yorktown, General Washington spent two more years commanding his soldiers before a final treaty was signed. He returned to Mount Vernon in 1783.

WHEN THE WAR ENDED, WASHINGTON RETIRED to Mount Vernon. He was happy to be home with his wife, able to enjoy life on the plantation once again. Washington expected to spend the rest of his life at home in Virginia. The office of the United States president would not be invented for six more years. He spent time with his wife, Martha, and her grandchildren. By this time, he and Martha had many responsibilities. They owned more than 200 slaves. The plantation stretched over 10 miles. Washington liked to visit each of Mount Vernon's five farms every day. He had 3,000 acres planted with crops, and he also raised cattle.

While Washington enjoyed his time at home, the new nation faced a crisis. Even before

the war ended, the 13 colonies had begun to call themselves states and formed a **union.** After much argument, they had approved the **Articles of Confederation.** This set up a central government. Americans were afraid to give a few men too much power, however. They did not want a strong Congress to make laws that everyone had to obey. Instead, each state was responsible for its own business. Each state collected its own taxes, issued its own money, built its own roads, and so forth.

George and Martha Washington loved their days together at Mount Vernon. They often spent time with Martha's grand-children. Many people wanted to meet the heroic former general, and the Washingtons often had guests.

The Articles of Confederation had joined the states together. Unfortunately, it provided them with no strong central government. Washington and other leaders feared that such independent states might cause the weak Union to fall apart. They decided that the Articles of Confederation should be replaced by a **constitution.**

As a result, the Constitutional Convention was held in Philadelphia. The members of the convention met to write the U.S. Constitution.

When Washington presided over the Constitutional Convention, he helped shape the nation's most important laws—the very foundation of American government.

They put Washington in charge by electing him as their chairman. He did not write the Constitution, but he led the convention meetings. By nature, Washington was a friendly, quiet, polite man. But in his years as a soldier, he also had showed himself to be strong-willed, stern, and fair. Men looked up to him as a leader.

Terrible arguments broke out between the **delegates** at the Constitutional Convention. Still, Washington realized that he and the other delegates were doing something amazing. "You will permit me to say that a greater drama is now acting on this theater than has heretofore been brought on the American stage, or any other in the world," Washington wrote in a letter. He believed it was an incredible honor for people to create their own government.

James Madison was a delegate to the Constitutional Convention. He took careful notes and saved them for future generations. Madison's notes provide much of what we know about that historic event. It was Madison who first suggested that the government should be divided into three parts: the executive, the judicial, and the legislative branches.

On September 17, 1787, representatives of 12 states signed the Constitution. This act turned the new nation into a **republic.** It established a federal government with three separate parts—the **executive, judicial,** and **legislative** branches. It established **checks and balances.** This made sure that no branch could have too much power. It even created the office of president.

The convention finally agreed on the Constitution. Now voters from at least nine states had to accept it. It took a full year for this to happen. Then Americans elected a Congress, which set up an **electoral college.** On February 4, 1789, the electoral college voted for a president. The ballots were counted on April 6. George Washington had won by **unanimous** vote.

George Washington learned that he had been elected president eight days later. He had not **campaigned** for the office, and he was not interested in **politics.** In fact, he said being the president would be the "greatest sacrifice of my personal feelings and wishes."

Even though he did not want to be president, Washington accepted the position. He believed it was his duty to continue to lead his country. It still seemed possible that the Union might fall apart one day. He was determined to keep that from happening.

AMERICANS REJOICED WHEN GEORGE WASHINGTON WAS ELECTED THE first president of the United States. In April of 1789, he left Mount Vernon in a carriage. He was bound for New York City on a journey that would take eight days. Washington worried that the American people might be unhappy about his election because he had once promised never to run for public office. His mind soon eased. All along the route, people turned out to cheer him. People shot off cannons and lit bonfires in his honor. When he reached the capital city of New York, he refused to get in a carriage, preferring to walk. As he went by, the people lining the streets fell silent and bowed to him.

President Washington took his oath of office on April 30. He stood outside on a balcony at Federal Hall. At the end of his oath, he added his own prayer, "so help me God." A huge crowd witnessed the event, and grand celebrations followed.

Chapter THREE

The Experiment

Washington once wrote that leaving Mount Vernon to become the president "was the greatest sacrifice I have ever … been called upon to make."

BECOMING PRESIDENT MEANT THAT GEORGE Washington had to leave Mount Vernon and depend on others to run his plantation. He moved to New York City, which was then the capital city of the United States. Martha Washington was very upset when he was elected. She had hoped they would spend the rest of their lives at Mount Vernon. She did not go to New York at first, but she joined him later.

George Washington was sworn in as the first president of the United States on April 30, 1789. In the months following his **inauguration,** President Washington spent most of his time getting the executive branch up and running. When he entered office, he and John Adams, his vice president, were the

only staff members in the executive branch. Congress had decided that the government should be divided into departments that would make up the rest of this branch. Washington had to choose men to head these departments, forming his **cabinet.** He appointed Thomas Jefferson as the secretary of state. Jefferson was in charge of U.S. relations with other countries. Alexander Hamilton, the secretary of the treasury, took care of the nation's **finances.** Washington named Edmund Randolph as the attorney general. Randolph was in charge of the country's legal matters. Henry Knox was the secretary of war, taking charge of

Two of Washington's most important advisors were Thomas Jefferson (left) and Alexander Hamilton (right). Unfortunately, Jefferson and Hamilton argued bitterly about many things. Hamilton believed that only rich landowners should be allowed to vote. Jefferson wanted to extend that right to more of the nation's population.

military issues. Washington also chose another 350 men to fill other, less important jobs.

George Washington set some important **precedents** that would affect how the American government works. He did not attend regular sessions of Congress. He gave Vice President Adams little to do. He decided to use his **veto** power only if Congress passed a law that he believed was **unconstitutional.** He never refused to sign a bill into law because of his personal feelings about it. Some later presidents would use their veto power differently, vetoing laws simply because they believed they were bad ideas. After the **Supreme Court** was established, it took the responsibility for deciding whether a law was unconstitutional.

Once Washington had gotten the government up and running, the biggest problem facing the nation was how to pay back money the states had

Washington is shown (at far right) with three members of his cabinet (left to right): Henry Knox, Thomas Jefferson, and Alexander Hamilton. Washington was determined not to choose friends, family, or the wealthy for his cabinet, but to choose men who he felt had the greatest reputations in the country.

borrowed to fight the Revolution. The government eventually settled the matter. It created a central bank that took over all the states' debts.

It was also during his first term that Washington decided where to locate the new national capital, which would be named Washington, D.C. While workers designed and built the city, the capital temporarily moved from New York to Philadelphia.

For a long time, Washington did not intend to run for a second term. He wanted to go home. He also had been hurt by some people's criticism of his manners. He thought it was important to create respect for the office of the president. To do so, he had attendants open doors and introduce him. He held many formal receptions. Some said such actions and activities were too much like those of a king. The American president was supposed to do things more simply. His feelings also had been hurt by people saying he had looked after his own interests when choosing where to build the nation's capital city. His own home was very close to the site chosen for Washington, D.C. Some

25

President Washington's government established the Bank of the United States to help pay the states' debts from the Revolutionary War.

said he wanted the capital there because it would bring money into Virginia—especially the area near Mount Vernon. This would mean Washington himself could make more money.

The election of February 1793 drew near. It seemed that most Americans still wanted Washington to be the president, even if some people criticized him. Unlike later presidents, Washington was not a member of a **political party.** He was not nominated by a group such as the Democrats or the Republicans. Instead, an individual nominated him for the office. Washington did not remove his name from the list of **candidates.**

In 1792, even though he longed to return to Mount Vernon, he was reelected by another unanimous vote of all 13 states.

Washington chose the location for the new nation's capital city. It was a plot of land on the Potomac River that covered about 10 square miles. He asked a famous French architect named Pierre L'Enfant to design the city.

Chapter FOUR

A Second Term

Washington is the only president to win an election by unanimous vote, and he did so twice.

DURING WASHINGTON'S SECOND TERM, he had to pay a great deal of attention to relations with other countries and with America's native peoples. Native Americans threatened settlers in the West. George Washington tried to make peace with them. He wanted to protect the Indians' rights to own land. He also wanted to keep them from siding with enemies of the United States, as they had in the French and Indian War.

The new nation was also trying to establish peaceful relations with Britain, Spain, and France. Washington believed the best thing for the United States to do about the European powers was to remain **neutral.** He decided that Americans should refuse to take sides in the disputes of other nations.

The U.S. government presented this medal to a Shawnee Indian chief, hoping it would encourage peace. The Indian chief is shown dropping his weapon, a tomahawk, and passing a peace pipe to President Washington.

One of Washington's great successes as president was to force Europeans from parts of the North American continent. Under Jay's Treaty, Britain gave up its forts in the Pacific Northwest. Spain still controlled the Mississippi River. That nation agreed to

Pinckney's Treaty, which allowed Americans to use their boats on the Mississippi. Now the United States could use the river to transport both people and goods across the continent and to the sea.

At home, an important event was the Whiskey Rebellion. Congress had passed a tax on whiskey. People living in western Pennsylvania threatened to revolt because they did not want to pay this tax.

President Washington took charge of 13,000 American troops during the Whiskey Rebellion. No president has ever led soldiers into action since.

Washington ordered the rebels "to retire peaceably to their homes." When they refused, he called out thousands of militia soldiers. He rode west to meet his new army. They settled the matter without bloodshed. Washington's actions showed American citizens that the states had to obey laws passed by the United States government.

In 1796, the American people wanted Washington to run for a third term, but he refused. He was beginning to feel old and wanted to retire. John Adams won the election and became the new president. In his farewell address, Washington told the nation his hopes and dreams for its future: "I shall carry to my grave the hope that your Union and brotherly affection may be perpetual; that the Constitution may be sacredly maintained; and that free government … the ever favorite object of my heart … will be the happy reward of our mutual cares, labors and danger."

George and Martha Washington went home to Mount Vernon to lead a happy, quiet life. Washington spent his time tending his farms and animals. Managing such a vast plantation took much of his energy.

Construction began on the Washington Monument in 1848, but the project was not completed for nearly 40 years. The Civil War and lack of funding halted construction. When it finally was finished in 1884, the monument stood more than 555 feet (169.2 meters) tall, making it the tallest building in the world at that time.

One day, Washington rode out in cold, wet weather and came down with a serious throat infection. The illness grew worse that evening, but he did not wake his wife or their servants. Within two days, the nation's first president was extremely ill. He died late at night on December 14, 1799. He was 67 years old.

Americans felt tremendous sorrow when they learned Washington had died. Congressman Harry Lee honored Washington as he spoke before Congress: "To the memory of the Man, first in war, first in peace, and first in the hearts of his countrymen."

Both the capital city and a state were named in George Washington's honor. In 1848, construction of the world-famous Washington Monument began. It would pay respect to both the first president and to the nation's capital. The monument stands as a towering reminder of Washington's enormous contributions to his country. The dollar bill and the quarter both bear his image. Schools, streets, bridges, and parks are named for Washington as well.

An entire nation continues to honor the man that many feel to be the greatest American president of all. Today Americans remember George Washington not only as our first president, but as the man who led his nation to independence.

GEORGE WASHINGTON LIVED IN A WORLD IN WHICH SLAVERY WAS accepted. When he was a child, his father owned slaves. As an adult, Washington inherited some slaves and bought others. The number of slaves at Mount Vernon also grew because Washington's slaves married and had children. Although Virginia law did not allow slaves to marry, Washington did recognize unions between husband and wife.

Still, Washington sometimes treated his slaves in a way that seems cruel today. For example, he sold a rebellious slave and used the profits to buy rum and food. Slaves worked from sun up until sun down, six days a week. Today many people cannot understand how a man who valued liberty and freedom ever could have owned slaves at all.

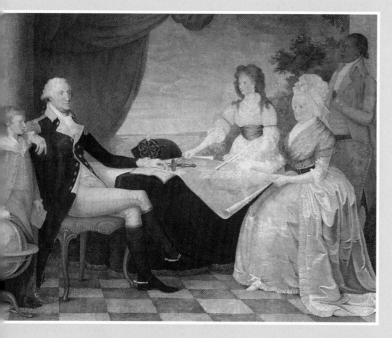

George and Martha Washington depended on slaves to work in the house and on the farms of Mount Vernon. Just before the Revolution, however, George Washington decided that he would no longer sell slaves without their consent. Although he stood by his word, his decision hurt him. As more slaves bore children and he switched to crops that required fewer people to

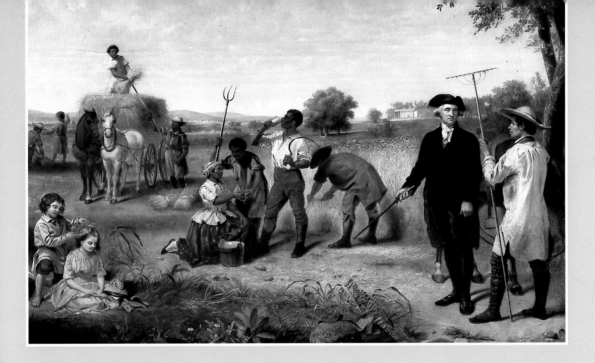

harvest them, he had to support more people than he needed. At one point, he had more than 300 slaves at Mount Vernon.

As he grew older, Washington felt more and more strongly that slavery was wrong, although he never pushed publicly for its end. Many Americans still believed in slavery at the time. If Washington had spoken out against it, he might never have been elected president. In 1793, Washington decided his goal would be to free all of his slaves, but he had not figured out how the ex-slaves could support themselves. He realized his family would have to support the children and the people who had become too old to work. He hoped neighboring farmers might be willing to hire the rest.

When Washington left the presidency in 1797, he left some slaves behind in Philadelphia, where the law freed them automatically. But he also smuggled others back to Mount Vernon rather than let them go free. Washington never did solve the problem of finding new employment for his slaves so he could free them. Still, his will freed about half of his slaves upon his death. Martha supported most of these people in the years that followed. The rest of the slaves had belonged to Martha when she and George married. These slaves still belonged to her after his death.

c. 1650 George Washington's ancestors arrive in the American colonies from England.

1732 On February 22, George Washington is born in Westmoreland County in Virginia. His parents, Augustine Washington and Mary Ball Washington, are farmers.

1743 Augustine Washington dies. After his death, 11-year-old George Washington goes to live at his half-brother Lawrence's home, called Mount Vernon.

1748 Still a teenager, George Washington goes along with his neighbors when they travel to the wild Shenandoah Valley to make a map of a piece of land they have purchased.

1749 Washington is appointed surveyor for Culpeper County, Virginia.

1751 George Washington sails to the Caribbean island of Barbados with Lawrence. It is the only time he will ever leave North America.

1752 When Lawrence Washington dies, George Washington joins the Virginia militia.

1753–1754 Washington is sent west by the governor of Virginia to stop the French from taking American lands in the Ohio Country. Soon the French and Indian War breaks out, in which Washington fights several battles.

1755 Washington takes part in an expedition against the French under the leadership of British General Edward Braddock. He is lucky to escape with his life and gains a reputation as an excellent soldier.

1759 After the end of the French and Indian War, George Washington returns to his plantation and marries Martha Dandridge Custis, a young widow with two children.

1761 George Washington inherits Mount Vernon.

1774 The colonists grow increasingly angry about Britain's taxation. They form the Continental Congress to unite and decide what to do. George Washington is elected to represent Virginia as a delegate to the First Continental Congress. At that time, few colonists are interested in independence from Britain.

1775 On April 19, the battles of Lexington and Concord take place, and the Revolution begins. Washington is appointed a member of the Second Continental Congress. On June 19, Congress appoints him commander of the colonists' Continental Army.

1776 The Continental Congress signs the Declaration of Independence on July 4, formally declaring the American colonies' independence from Britain. France begins to secretly send weapons and money to the Americans. On Christmas Eve, George Washington and his soldiers cross the Delaware River in the middle of the night to surprise the enemy in what will be known as the Battle of Trenton, the first American victory.

1777 After wins at Brandywine Creek and Germantown, Washington and his army suffer through a long, cold winter at Valley Forge.

1778 France joins the Revolution on the side of the patriots, and the tide begins to turn in favor of the Americans.

1781 After the Battle of Yorktown, British General Cornwallis surrenders on October 19. This ends the American Revolution.

1783 British troops leave the continent in November, more than two years after their surrender. American soldiers complain that they still have not received the promised pay for their time in the military. Washington secures a promise from Congress that the soldiers who fought in the Revolution will receive the pay they are owed. Washington resigns his commission as commander in chief and is finally able to go home. He is delighted to return to Mount Vernon.

1786 Many Americans express dissatisfaction with the Articles of Confederation. Washington corresponds with other leaders to decide what should be done.

1787 Leaders decide to create a constitution to replace the Articles of Confederation. Washington is elected president of the Constitutional Convention, which takes place from May to September. In the fall, delegates sign the Constitution and send it to be accepted by the states.

1789 On February 4, George Washington is elected the first president of the United States. He is inaugurated in New York City, the nation's capital city, on April 30. He selects the first presidential cabinet.

1790 Congress selects a permanent place for the U.S. capital city, a site along the Potomac River suggested by President Washington.

1792 Washington is reelected as president.

1794 The Whiskey Rebellion breaks out when farmers in Pennsylvania pick up arms in protest of a tax the government has placed on alcohol. George Washington rides to Pennsylvania to assume control of the American army but then resolves the conflict without bloodshed. In Jay's Treaty, Britain gives up its posts in what will become the American Pacific Northwest.

1795 Pinckney's Treaty opens the Mississippi River to American boats, allowing the transport of goods and people up and down the river.

1796 The American public hopes George Washington will run for a third term as president, but he refuses to allow his name to appear on the ballot.

1797 President Washington's second term comes to an end. He gives a famous farewell speech. John Adams, Washington's vice president, becomes the second president of the United States.

1799 On December 14, George Washington dies at Mount Vernon. The nation mourns his death.

allies (AL-lize)
Allies are nations that have agreed to help each other, for example, by fighting together against a common enemy. The United States and France were allies during the American Revolution.

ammunition (am-yuh-NISH-en)
Ammunition is bullets, cannonballs, and other things that can be exploded or fired from guns. Americans began to stockpile ammunition before the Revolution began.

Articles of Confederation (AR-teh-kelz OF kun-fed-uh-RAY-shun)
The Articles of Confederation made up the first plan for a central U.S. government. Under the Articles of Confederation, there was no president or national leader, but only a Congress.

cabinet (KAB-eh-net)
A cabinet is the group of people who advise a president. George Washington appointed his cabinet soon after he became president.

campaign (kam-PAYN)
If people campaign, they take part in activities, such as giving speeches, in the hope of winning an election. George Washington did not campaign to become the president of the United States.

candidates (KAN-deh-dats)
Candidates are people who are running in an election. Several candidates run for president every four years.

checks and balances (CHEKS AND BAL-en-sez)
Checks and balances are the limits the Constitution places on the branches of the federal government. For example, the president is commander in chief of the army, but only Congress can declare a war. Checks and balances prevent any one branch from becoming too powerful.

commission (kuh-MISH-en)
A commission is a position of power that is given to a person by the government or another authority. George Washington received a commission to become the commander of the Continental Army.

constitution (kon-stih-TOO-shun)
A constitution is the set of basic principles that govern a state, country, or society. The U.S. Constitution describes the way the United States is governed.

**Continental Army
(kon-tuh-NEN-tul AR-mee)**
The Continental Army was the American army that fought in the Revolution. George Washington was the general of the Continental Army.

**Continental Congress
(kon-tuh-NEN-tul KONG-gris)**
The Continental Congress was the group of men who governed the United States during and after the Revolution. George Washington was a member of the Continental Congress.

delegates (DEL-uh-gitz)
Delegates are people who are elected by others to take part in something. Each colony sent delegates to the Continental Congress.

**electoral college
(ee-LEKT-uh-rul KOL-ij)**
The electoral college is made up of representatives from each state who vote for candidates in presidential elections. Members of the electoral college cast their votes based on what most people in their state want.

executive (eg-ZEK-yuh-tiv)
An executive manages things or makes decisions. The executive branch of the U.S. government includes the president and the cabinet members.

expedition (ek-speh-DISH-un)
An expedition is a journey made for a special purpose. George Washington took part in an expedition to find out whether the French were building forts on British land.

finances (FYE-nan-siz)
Finances are the money and income that a person, country, or company has. The secretary of treasury is in charge of the nation's finances.

**inauguration
(ih-naw-gyuh-RAY-shun)**
An inauguration is the ceremony that takes place when a new president begins a term of office. George Washington's first inauguration was in New York City.

judicial (joo-DISH-ul)
Judicial means relating to courts of law. The judicial branch of the U.S. government includes its courts and judges.

legislative (LEJ-uh-slay-tiv)
Legislative means having to do with the making of laws. The legislative branch of the U.S. government is Congress, and Congress makes the nation's laws.

militia (muh-LISH-uh)
A militia is a volunteer army, made up of citizens who have trained as soldiers. Virginia had a militia for times of emergency.

neutral (NOO-trul)
If a country is neutral, it does not take sides. George Washington believed the United States should remain neutral, rather than take sides in European wars.

plantation (plan-TAY-shun)
A plantation is a large farm or group of farms. Mount Vernon was the name of George Washington's plantation.

**political party
(puh-LIT-uh-kul PAR-tee)**
A political party is a group of people who share similar ideas about how to run a government. Today the two major U.S. political parties are the Democratic and Republican parties.

politics (PAWL-uh-tiks)
Politics refers to the actions and practices of the government. George Washington did not have a natural interest in politics.

precedents (PRES-uh-dentz)
Precedents are actions that later serve as examples for others to follow. When presidents purposely try to act as George Washington would have, they follow his precedents.

**representative
(rep-ree-ZEN-tuh-tiv)**
A representative is someone who attends a meeting, having agreed to speak or act for others. Congress is made up of representatives elected by the American people.

republic (ree-PUB-lik)
A republic is a nation in which citizens elect representatives to their central government. The United States became a republic after the Constitution was approved.

retreat (ree-TREET)
If an army retreats, it moves back or withdraws to avoid danger or defeat. The Continental Army retreated to Pennsylvania.

revolution (rev-uh-LOO-shun)
A revolution is something that causes a complete change in government. The American Revolution was a war fought between the United States and England.

Supreme Court
(suh-PREEM KORT)
The Supreme Court is the most powerful court in the United States. The Supreme Court decides if laws are unconstitutional.

surrender (suh-REN-dur)
If an army surrenders, it gives up to the enemy. When British General Cornwallis surrendered, he promised his soldiers would no longer fight with the Americans.

surveyor (sur-VAY-ur)
A surveyor is a person who determines the boundaries of a piece of land. Surveyors used to make maps of a property while they measured it.

treaty (TREE-tee)
A treaty is a formal agreement made between nations. The United States and England signed a peace treaty after the American Revolution ended.

unanimous (yoo-NAN-uh-mess)
If something is unanimous, everybody agrees on it. Because every member of the electoral college voted for George Washington, their vote was unanimous.

unconstitutional
(un-kon-stih-TOO-shuh-nul)
If something is unconstitutional, it goes against the Constitution of the United States. The Supreme Court decides whether laws are unconstitutional.

union (YOO-nyen)
A union is the joining together of two or more people or groups of people, such as states. The United States is also known as the Union.

veto (VEE-toh)
A veto is the president's power to refuse to sign a bill into law. Unless a large majority in Congress votes to overrule the veto, the bill does not become law.

President	Birthplace	Life Span	Presidency	Political Party	First Lady
George Washington	Virginia	1732–1799	1789–1797	None	Martha Dandridge Custis Washington
John Adams	Massachusetts	1735–1826	1797–1801	Federalist	Abigail Smith Adams
Thomas Jefferson	Virginia	1743–1826	1801–1809	Democratic-Republican	widower
James Madison	Virginia	1751–1836	1809–1817	Democratic Republican	Dolley Payne Todd Madison
James Monroe	Virginia	1758–1831	1817–1825	Democratic Republican	Elizabeth Kortright Monroe
John Quincy Adams	Massachusetts	1767–1848	1825–1829	Democratic-Republican	Louisa Johnson Adams
Andrew Jackson	South Carolina	1767–1845	1829–1837	Democrat	widower
Martin Van Buren	New York	1782–1862	1837–1841	Democrat	widower
William H Harrison	Virginia	1773–1841	1841	Whig	Anna Symmes Harrison
John Tyler	Virginia	1790–1862	1841–1845	Whig	Letitia Christian Tyler / Julia Gardiner Tyler
James K. Polk	North Carolina	1795–1849	1845–1849	Democrat	Sarah Childress Polk

President	Birthplace	Life Span	Presidency	Political Party	First Lady
Zachary Taylor	Virginia	1784–1850	1849–1850	Whig	Margaret Mackall Smith Taylor
Millard Fillmore	New York	1800–1874	1850–1853	Whig	Abigail Powers Fillmore
Franklin Pierce	New Hampshire	1804–1869	1853–1857	Democrat	Jane Means Appleton Pierce
James Buchanan	Pennsylvania	1791–1868	1857–1861	Democrat	never married
Abraham Lincoln	Kentucky	1809–1865	1861–1865	Republican	Mary Todd Lincoln
Andrew Johnson	North Carolina	1808–1875	1865–1869	Democrat	Eliza McCardle Johnson
Ulysses S. Grant	Ohio	1822–1885	1869–1877	Republican	Julia Dent Grant
Rutherford B. Hayes	Ohio	1822–1893	1877–1881	Republican	Lucy Webb Hayes
James A. Garfield	Ohio	1831–1881	1881	Republican	Lucretia Rudolph Garfield
Chester A. Arthur	Vermont	1829–1886	1881–1885	Republican	widower
Grover Cleveland	New Jersey	1837–1908	1885–1889	Democrat	Frances Folsom Cleveland

President	Birthplace	Life Span	Presidency	Political Party	First Lady
Benjamin Harrison	Ohio	1833–1901	1889–1893	Republican	Caroline Scott Harrison
Grover Cleveland	New Jersey	1837–1908	1893–1897	Democrat	Frances Folsom Cleveland
William McKinley	Ohio	1843–1901	1897–1901	Republican	Ida Saxton McKinley
Theodore Roosevelt	New York	1858–1919	1901–1909	Republican	Edith Kermit Carow Roosevelt
William H. Taft	Ohio	1857–1930	1909–1913	Republican	Helen Herron Taft
Woodrow Wilson	Virginia	1856–1924	1913–1921	Democrat	Ellen L. Axson Wilson / Edith Bolling Galt Wilson
Warren G. Harding	Ohio	1865–1923	1921–1923	Republican	Florence Kling De Wolfe Harding
Calvin Coolidge	Vermont	1872–1933	1923–1929	Republican	Grace Goodhue Coolidge
Herbert C. Hoover	Iowa	1874–1964	1929–1933	Republican	Lou Henry Hoover
Franklin D. Roosevelt	New York	1882–1945	1933–1945	Democrat	Anna Eleanor Roosevelt Roosevelt
Harry S. Truman	Missouri	1884–1972	1945–1953	Democrat	Elizabeth Wallace Truman

Our PRESIDENTS

President	Birthplace	Life Span	Presidency	Political Party	First Lady
Dwight D. Eisenhower	Texas	1890–1969	1953–1961	Republican	Mary "Mamie" Doud Eisenhower
John F. Kennedy	Massachusetts	1917–1963	1961–1963	Democrat	Jacqueline Bouvier Kennedy
Lyndon B. Johnson	Texas	1908–1973	1963–1969	Democrat	Claudia Alta Taylor Johnson
Richard M. Nixon	California	1913–1994	1969–1974	Republican	Thelma Catherine Ryan Nixon
Gerald Ford	Nebraska	1913–	1974–1977	Republican	Elizabeth "Betty" Bloomer Warren Ford
James Carter	Georgia	1924–	1977–1981	Democrat	Rosalynn Smith Carter
Ronald Reagan	Illinois	1911–	1981–1989	Republican	Nancy Davis Reagan
George Bush	Massachusetts	1924–	1989–1993	Republican	Barbara Pierce Bush
William Clinton	Arkansas	1946–	1993–2001	Democrat	Hillary Rodham Clinton
George W. Bush	Connecticut	1946–	2001–	Republican	Laura Welch Bush

Presidential FACTS

Qualifications
To run for president, a candidate must
- be at least 35 years old
- be a citizen who was born in the United States
- have lived in the United States for 14 years

Term of Office
A president's term of office is four years. No president can stay in office for more than two terms.

Election Date
The presidential election takes place every four years on the first Tuesday of November.

Inauguration Date
Presidents are inaugurated on January 20.

Oath of Office
I do solemnly swear I will faithfully execute the office of the President of the United States and will to the best of my ability preserve, protect, and defend the Constitution of the United States.

Write a Letter to the President
One of the best things about being a U.S. citizen is that Americans get to participate in their government. They can speak out if they feel government leaders aren't doing their jobs. They can also praise leaders who are going the extra mile. Do you have something you'd like the president to do? Should the president worry more about the environment and encourage people to recycle? Should the government spend more money on our schools? You can write a letter to the president to say how you feel!

1600 Pennsylvania Avenue
Washington, D.C. 20500

You can even send an e-mail to: president@whitehouse.gov

Internet Sites

Learn more about George Washington as a surveyor:
http://www.loc.gov/exhibits/treasures/tr010.html

Learn more about George Washington's life and see his papers:
http://www.virginia.edu/gwpapers/

Learn more about George Washington as a child:
http://www.loc.gov/exhibits/treasures/trr048.html

Learn more about the American Revolution:
http://www.pbs.org/ktca/liberty/

Tour Mount Vernon at:
http://www.mountvernon.org

Learn more about all the presidents and visit the White House:
http://www.whitehouse.gov/WH/glimpse/presidents/html/presidents.html
http://www.thepresidency.org/presinfo.htm
http://www.americanpresidents.org

Books

Feinberg, Barbara Silberdick. *America's First Ladies.* Danbury, CT: Franklin Watts, 1998.

Rosenburg, John. *First in War: George Washington in the American Revolution.* Brookfield, CT: Millbrook Press, 1998.

Rosenburg, John. *First in Peace: George Washington, the Constitution, and the Presidency.* Brookfield, CT: Millbrook Press, 1998.

Rubel, David. *Scholastic Encyclopedia of the Presidents and Their Times.* New York: Scholastic, 1994.

Index

Adams, John, 22, 31, 37
American Revolution, 12-14, 16, 25, 36
Articles of Confederation, 17-18, 37

Bank of the United States, 26
Battle of Trenton, 14, 36
Battle of Yorktown, 37
Battles of Lexington and Concord, 36
bills, signing into law, 24
Braddock, Edward, 36
British, 9-10, 12-14, 29, 37
    taxation by, 11
    and Revolution, 12-14

cabinet, presidential, 23-24
central bank, 25, 26
checks and balances, 19-20
Congress, 20, 30, 37
Constitution, 18-20, 31, 37
Constitutional Convention, 18-19, 37
Continental Army, 12, 14, 36
Continental Congress, 11, 17, 36
Cornwallis, General, 14, 37
Custis, Martha. *See* Washington, Martha

Declaration of Independence, 36

executive branch, 19, 22-23

Federal Hall, 21
Ferry Farm, 6
French, 9-10, 14, 36, 37
French and Indian War, 10, 13, 28, 36

government, central, 17-20, 23, 31

Hamilton, Alexander, 23
House of Burgesses, 11

Jay's Treaty, 29, 37
Jefferson, Thomas, 23-24
judicial branch, 19

Knox, Henry, 23-24

laws, unconstitutional, 24
Lee, Harry, 33
legislative branch, 19
L'Enfant, Pierre, 27

Madison, James, 19
militia, 8, 10, 30, 36
Mississippi River, 29, 37
Mount Vernon, 7, 8, 15, 16-17, 22, 31, 36-37
    slaves at, 34-35

Native Americans, 10, 28-29

Ohio River valley expedition, 9, 36

Philadelphia, 18, 25, 35
Pinckney's Treaty, 29, 37
political parties, 26, 33
Potomac River, 7, 15, 27
president, office of, 20, 25

Randolph, Edmund, 23

slavery, 7, 16, 34-35
Supreme Court, 24

taxation, 11, 30

Valley Forge, 37
veto power, 24

Washington, Augustine, 6-7, 36
Washington, D.C., 25-27
Washington, George
    cherry tree incident, 8
    death of, 32-33, 37
    farewell address, 31, 33, 37
    inauguration of, 21-22, 37
    land ownership of, 8, 10-11, 33
    national tributes to, 32-33
    reelection of, 26-27, 37
    second term, 28-35
    slaves of, 7, 16, 34-35
Washington, Lawrence, 7-8, 13, 36
Washington, Martha, 10-11, 16-17, 22, 31, 33-35
Washington, Mary Bell, 7, 36
Washington Monument, 32-33
Weems, Mason, 8
Whiskey Rebellion, 30-31, 37

Yorktown, surrender at, 14